The World's Best Mother-in-Law Jokes

07/2

Des MacHale

The World's Best Mother-in-Law Jokes

Illustrations by Louis Silvestro

ANGUS
& ROBERTSON
PUBLISHERS

ANGUS & ROBERTSON PUBLISHERS

*Unit 4, Eden Park, 31 Waterloo Road,
North Ryde, NSW, Australia 2113, and
16 Golden Square, London W1R 4BN,
United Kingdom*

*First published in Australia
by Angus & Robertson Publishers in 1987
First published in the United Kingdom
by Angus & Robertson (UK) in 1987
Reprinted 1987*

*Published by arrangement with
The Mercier Press Ltd, Cork, Ireland*

*Text copyright © Des MacHale 1987
Illustrations copyright © Louis Silvestro 1987*

*National Library of Australia
Cataloguing-in-publication data.*

*MacHale, Des.
   The world's best mother-in-law jokes.
   ISBN 0 207 15466 X.*

*1. English wit and humor. I. Silvestro, Louis.
   1953-   . II. Title*
828'.91402

*Typeset in 12 pt Goudy Old Style Bold by Setrite Typesetters
Printed in the United Kingdom*

INTRODUCTION

For thousands of years, weak-willed and spineless men have trembled in fear of the most fearsome and ferocious of all creations — the mother-in-law. Then, around the turn of the century, music-hall comedians uncovered a new weapon — the mother-in-law joke — as a feeble comeback. The stereotype mother-in-law emerged as a monster weighing as much as two elephants; a nightmare in curlers with a personality that would make Attila the Hun look like a choirboy.

This book is a celebration of that neglected art form, the mother-in-law joke, and is to be taken in small doses three times a day by hen-pecked sons-in-law until the homicidal tendencies pass. But be warned, under no circumstances must it be allowed to pass into the hands of your mother-in-law — that woman has quite enough ammunition against you already!

A man had just become engaged and was visiting his future mother-in-law for the first time.

"How old do you think I am?" she asked, a strange smile playing on her lips.

The young man thought for a moment and then proved himself wise beyond his years.

"Well Ma'am," he responded with what appeared like perfect gravity, "I'm wondering whether to make you ten years younger to fit in with your looks, or ten years older on account of your intelligence."

My mother-in-law once got a job on a farm but left it after a couple of weeks. She got fed up standing out in a field in all weathers with her arms outstretched. I'll say this for her though, the birds came and brought back the grain they had stolen the previous year.

Behind every successful man is a mother-in-law telling him he's a failure.

Sophia Loren — take away her looks and figure and what have you got? My mother-in-law.

A young man who had recently been married had not learned all the ropes of matrimony. He consulted a married friend.

"I simply don't know what to call my mother-in-law. Since my own mother is still living, it doesn't seem right to call my wife's mother 'Mother'."

"Oh, that's easy," his friend said. "I had the same problem. At first I addressed her as 'Hey', but now I just use a simple 'Sir'."

My mother-in-law is away on holiday but three times a week I have a woman come in and nag me.

I'm not saying my mother-in-law is tough, but when she eats sardines she doesn't bother to open the tin.

Flanigan: "My mother-in-law has just eloped with my best friend."

Lanigan: "What was his name?"

Flanigan: "I don't know. I've never met the fellow."

There had been a disaster. The dead and injured were brought to a makeshift hospital and lay side by side. One of those believed dead was accompanied by his mother-in-law who was anxious to claim the insurance.

She asked a doctor, "He is dead, isn't he?"

"Yes, yes," replied the harassed doctor, assuming that all in that particular row were dead.

At that moment, the son-in-law suddenly sat up in the stretcher and moaned, "I'm not dead, doc."

"Lie down," snapped his mother-in-law. "The doctor knows best."

My mother-in-law wanted to have her mind lifted so she applied for a brain transplant. The brain rejected her.

If there is anything that a mother-in-law does not know, she imagines it.

I'm not saying my mother-in-law is a bad cook, but she's the only woman I know whose dustbin has ulcers.

An Englishman to his friend: "I'm going to see my mother-in-law in New York."
Friend: "I thought she lived in London."
Englishman: "She does, but she looks better from New York."

The first time I met my mother-in-law I thought she was wearing sunglasses. But it was just the way her nostrils looked when she got angry.

The husband was expecting his wife home from a holiday at her mother's. When he saw both his wife and his mother-in-law walking up the path, he took his wife aside and whispered to her: "Didn't I telegraph you not to bring back your mother with you?"

"Yes, that's what she's here to see you about."

My mother-in-law is so ugly you have to be over eighteen to be allowed to look at her. Even her home movies are X-rated.

I'm not saying my mother-in-law has a big mouth, but when she smiles she gets lipstick on both her ears. She's the only woman I know who can eat a banana sideways.

How can we be sure Adam lived in Paradise? He had no mother-in-law.

Husband to wife: "When I see your mother coming up the garden path, dear, I sometimes wish I had loved and lost."

"I've just come to tell you that I think you're a great man of medicine," beamed the young man on entering the doctor's surgery. "I've benefited so much from your treatment!"

The doctor was speechless with confusion for a few seconds. "But you're not one of my patients."

"No," said the young man, "but my mother-in-law was. I've just come from the funeral."

A newly-married man was telling his friend about a fight he had just had with his mother-in-law.

"Look, swallow your pride," his friend advised. "Admit you were wrong and apologise to her."

The young man replied angrily, "You haven't been listening! I was the one who was in the right; she was wrong. Even my wife agrees with me."

"Oh, I see!" said the friend. "In that case I'd take her a box of chocolates as well."

Winding up with a nice mother-in-law is like putting your hand into a bag of snakes in the hope of drawing out an eel.

Only one man ever took a deep interest in my mother-in-law, and he was a vet.

My mother-in-law is pretty fat. Once she was paddling by the seaside when a beach guard asked her if she would mind coming out because the tide wouldn't come in.

Then she got this terrific job. She's the decoy for a whaling fleet.

I left my wife because of another woman — her mother.

At the aquarium, a man was being chased by a middle-aged woman brandishing a rolling pin. In desperation he jumped into the shark pool. Bobbing to the surface, surrounded by circling fins, he yelled, "For God's sake mother-in-law, go away!"

She shouted back: "Come out of there and take your punishment, you lily-livered coward!"

My mother-in-law has a red head. No hair, just a red head.

A farmer was milking a cow when a bull began to charge from the other end of the field.

"Watch out," yelled a farmhand, but the farmer just sat there milking away as the bull came closer and closer. When it was only a couple of metres away, the bull stopped suddenly and ran madly back to where it had come from.

"What on earth did you do to him?" the farmhand asked.

"Nothing," smiled the farmer. "I just happen to know that this cow is his mother-in-law."

I'm not saying my mother-in-law is fat, but she can answer the front door without leaving the kitchen.

Two cannibals after a hunting trip were sitting outside their hut, about to commence their evening meal.

As they hacked away at the poor victim's torso in readiness for the feast, one remarked: "Do you know what, I hate my mother-in-law's guts."

"Don't let that worry you," the other replied. "Push them aside and eat your vegies first."

My mother-in-law has a disgusting habit — she comes to visit me.

It's all my own fault. I should never have taken that thorn out of my mother-in-law's paw.

Every happy event in life has a snag, as the man said when his mother-in-law died and he had to pay the funeral expenses.

My mother-in-law speaks through her nose. She has to — her mouth is worn out.

Mother-in-law was ill in bed when the doctor came. Placing a thermometer in her mouth, the doctor said, "Don't open your mouth for fifteen minutes."

Afterwards, the son-in-law took the doctor aside and whispered, "Look, doc, how much do you want for that thing?"

My mother-in-law saves a lot of money by making her own yoghurt. She just puts a pint of milk on the mantelpiece and stares at it.

Two grey-coiffed matrons were talking.

"I thought you couldn't stand him, Muriel," Marigold exclaimed. "I was so surprised when you allowed your daughter to marry him..."

"You're right," Muriel broke in, an evil glint in her eye, "I just wanted to be his mother-in-law for a while."

My mother-in-law suffers from crow's feet, but she keeps her shoes on and nobody notices.

A man was tried and found guilty of attempting to murder his mother-in-law. Passing sentence, His Honour smiled at the prisoner and said, "For this crime you must be punished. But I am going to be lenient with you and not imprison you. I shall fine you half your week's wages and send you home a free man."

Later, a colleague asked the judge why he had been so lenient.

"Ah," said the judge, "I've always believed in giving a man a second chance."

Then there was the fellow who saw a sign: "Keep Your Country Beautiful". So he went home and shot his mother-in-law.

When Flanigan died he went to hell, but within a few weeks he made such a nuisance of himself down there that the devil considered throwing him out.

"Look," he told Flanigan, "you're behaving as if you owned the place."

"Why shouldn't I?" said Flanigan. "After all, my mother-in-law gave it to me before I died."

I'm not saying my mother-in-law is ugly, it's just that she's got this terrible birthmark between her ears. Recently, she had some work done on her nose — they've moved it in between her eyes. Then she had her face lifted, but when they saw what was underneath they put everything back again.

My mother-in-law has a slight speech impediment — every so often she pauses to breathe.

The woman was overjoyed. Her daughter, a missionary in a remote part of Africa, had just sent word of her impending marriage. She immediately started gossiping about it to her friends, telling them her only daughter was about to marry an extremely wealthy medical practitioner.

A few weeks after the wedding, the mother decided to journey to Africa to visit her daughter and new son-in-law.

To her horror, she found her daughter living in a small, filthy mud hut in the depths of the jungle. Standing next to her was a huge native, whose naked body was tattooed all over with the most obscene patterns imaginable. He wore a wild boar's head for a hat and there was a necklace of shrunken human heads hanging around his neck. A pile of human skulls and bones lay behind him.

When she learned that this man was her new son-in-law, she promptly fainted. Her last words were: "Oh Lord! I thought you said you were marrying a *rich* doctor..."

Mick was quietly crying into his beer when Pat joined him at the bar.

"The fight with your mother-in-law didn't go well eh?" asked Pat.

"She came *crawling* to me on her *knees*," Mick declared.

"What did she say?"

"'Come out from under the bed you snivelling little coward!'"

My mother-in-law does a bit of singing. Yesterday she was practising and three factories knocked off for lunch.

My mother-in-law bought me two ties for Christmas — a red one and a green one. On Christmas morning I came down to breakfast wearing the red tie, just to please her.

"What's the matter with the green one then?" she snarled.

My mother-in-law boasts that she is a self-made woman. That certainly relieves the Almighty of a dreadful responsibility.

I'm not saying my mother-in-law is a fast eater, but it's the only time I've ever seen racing colours on a knife and fork.

I was travelling on a bus the other day when the conductor said, "You've had a row with your mother-in-law, haven't you?"

"How the hell did you know that?" I asked him.

"You've still got an axe stuck in your head."

Caspar Milquetoast, a meek little fellow with thick glasses, bandy legs and a nervous, whispery voice, had been charged with murdering his mother-in-law.

"Why did you do it, Caspar?" demanded the police inspector. "You, an upstanding citizen. Why did you kill your mother-in-law?"

"Well," said Caspar in a quavering voice, "she had her back to me, her glasses off, she was bending over, there was a bread knife handy, and the back door was open for a quick getaway."

Social etiquette is when you make your mother-in-law feel at home when you wish she was.

I'm not saying my mother-in-law is unattractive, but she couldn't lure a man out of a burning building.

Two friends were talking at a bus stop.

"You look shaken, Bob. What's the matter?"

"I had to admit an old school friend of mine to a mental home," said Bob, beads of sweat popping up on his forehead. "It's all so sickeningly awful!"

"Yes," nodded his friend, "mental illness is such a tragic thing. What exactly happened?"

"Well, he married a gorgeous young girl and went to live with her in her mother's house. Within a month their marriage was on the rocks."

"A month?" said the other, incredulously. "He had a nervous breakdown then?"

Bob, deathly pale, sweating profusely, clutching his stomach as a wave of nausea swept over him, was barely able to reply. "Yes," he finally breathed. "He'd decided that he loved his mother-in-law and couldn't stand the sight of his wife."

Actually, a man cannot legally marry his mother-in-law. Honest, it's on the statute books, but then there are lots of other unnecessary laws on the books too.

Flanigan's mother-in-law went missing so he reported her to the police as a missing person.

"Can you give us an exact description," said the policeman, getting out notebook and pencil.

"Well," said Flanigan, "she's about thirty, blond and has a 38-24-38 figure."

"Hold on a moment," said the policeman. "I've seen your mother-in-law and I'm sure she's over sixty-five, almost bald and about as big as a house."

"Of course she is," said Flanigan, "but would you want a fright like that back?"

"When did she disappear?" The law licked his pencil.

"About a month ago," Flanigan recalled.

"Why didn't you report it sooner?"

"Well," said Flanigan, "for three weeks I thought I was just having a pleasant dream."

My mother-in-law has everything a man could desire — big muscles, a hairy chest and a huge moustache.

A policeman on the beat in a public park came across a man crying uncontrollably on a bench.

When asked to explain the man said that once he had contemplated killing his mother-in-law but that his lawyer had advised him against it, saying that he would get twenty-five years in prison.

"Just think," he sobbed, "tonight I would have been a free man."

I'm not saying my mother-in-law is ugly, but her first child refused to breastfeed from her until she covered up her face.

The minister was asking questions of children at the Sunday school.

"Who is it, young fellow, before whom we all tremble and before whom even I am a worm?"

The boy's face darkened as he replied in hushed tones: "The missus's mother, sir."

My mother-in-law is one of a pair of twins, but it's easy to tell them apart. Her brother doesn't have a beard.

What is the definition of mixed emotions? Watching your mother-in-law drive over a cliff in your new car.

Flanigan walked into the fire station and reported that his mother-in-law was missing.

"Sorry," said the fire chief, "but we can't help you. Why don't you try the police station?"

"No fear," said Flanigan. "Last time she went missing, I went there and they found her."

I'm not saying my mother-in-law is ugly, but the local peeping Tom called round the other day and asked her if she would mind closing the curtains.

My mother-in-law is so fat that when she tried skipping it registered 7 on the Richter scale. She's the only woman I know who is taller lying down than standing up.

Sometimes I'm kind to my mother-in-law. For example, last Christmas I bought her a bottle opener because it used to upset me watching her opening beer bottles with her teeth.

Grimthorpe-Smythe, retired big-game hunter, was entertaining friends in his study with tales of his days in India.

He pointed to the skin of a tiger on the floor, "In spite of my well-known views on the protection of endangered species, I had to shoot that animal. When I saw him between the sights of my gun, I knew it was either him or me."

As he was speaking, his mother-in-law entered the room and observed, "If only the tiger had shot first."

Have you heard about Marriage Anonymous, the new association for bachelors? If you feel tempted to get married, they send you over a mother-in-law in a dressing gown and hair curlers.

My mother-in-law is so big that we have to grease the bath to get her in. Even then she can't take a bath because there's no room for the water.

My mother-in-law claims I'm effeminate. Compared to her, I probably am.

I'm not saying my mother-in-law is old, but when organ transplants first came out she put her name down for one of everything.

And lie about her age! According to my calculations she was only six when her first child was born.

Gerald came home drunk one night and began to insult his mother-in-law.

"You're the ugliest woman I've ever seen," he roared at her.

"And you're the drunkest man I've ever seen," she roared back.

"Maybe so," said Gerald, "but at least tomorrow I'll be sober."

My mother-in-law looks like a million dollars — all green and wrinkled.

Flanigan's mother-in-law has a figure like a million dollars, too — in loose change.

My mother-in-law went to a computer dating agency. She was told her ideal mate had been extinct for four million years.

A family visiting a park were just passing the wishing well when, suddenly, in toppled the mother-in-law.

Her son-in-law was quiet for a moment and then admitted, "I didn't think this damned thing still worked."

Norm was ensconced on his lounge, watching footie with a can of beer in one hand, a cigarette in the other and a couple of meat pies nearby. His mother-in-law walked in and glared at him disapprovingly.

"Oh, come on Ma," he smiled, "you can't really believe I'm *enjoying* myself!"

I hate my mother-in-law. Of course I'm aware that but for her I wouldn't have my wife. And that's another reason I hate her.

I'm not saying my mother-in-law is a big woman, but an admirer once drank champagne from her shoe — four and a half gallons at one go.

I'm not saying my mother-in-law is ugly, but she looks like something a body snatcher threw back.

My mother-in-law has a very clean mind. She should have, she changes it every ten minutes.

Wonderful woman my mother-in-law — eighty-nine years old and never uses glasses. She drinks straight from the bottle.

A woman reported the disappearance of her husband to the police.

"Is there any message you'd like us to give your husband if we find him?" asked the kindly sergeant.

"Yes," she replied. "Tell him mother didn't come after all."

M y mother-in-law is so fat that she puts her make-up on with a paint roller.

T hey had been fighting for weeks. George, at last, decided to have a heart-to-heart talk with his wife.

"Your mother has now been living with us for seven years, and she's driving me up the wall. I can't stand it any longer! I think it's about time she moved out and found a home of her own."

His wife stared at him in amazement. "My mother?" she cried. "I thought she was *your* mother."

My mother-in-law is so ugly that she spends four hours in the beauty salon just to get an estimate. When she goes in for treatment they cancel all leave and the staff get danger money.

A friend's mother-in-law always says she feels sick, even when she feels fine, just in case she feels worse the next day.

I'm not saying my mother-in-law looks like a witch, but she could look like one if she tidied herself up a bit. In our neighbourhood just to look at her is regarded as a cure for hiccups.

"Mean! There's no one her equal," said the customer, describing his mother-in-law to the barman. "The rooster died last month and we got nothing but chicken soup for a week. Then one of her cows died and we had beef stew for a fortnight. Me and the wife left the morning her husband died."

After I got married I said to my mother-in-law, "My house is your house." A week later she sold it.

I'm not saying my mother-in-law is a big woman, but when her husband carried her over the threshold he had to make three trips.

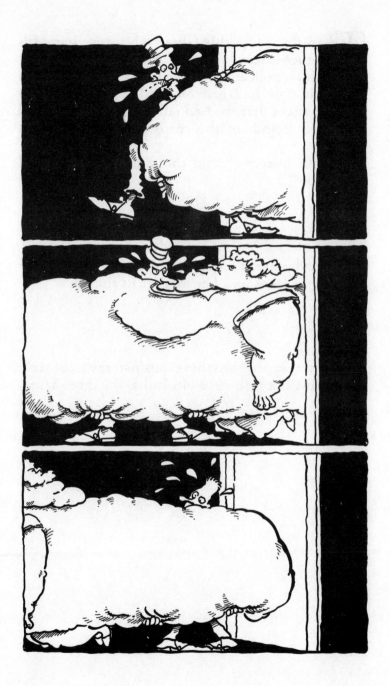

Then there was this fellow who was giving his mother-in-law a lift in the back of his car. Suddenly, a policeman flagged him down and told him that they had just received a phone call informing them that she had fallen out of the car and had been found on the roadside in the previous town.

"Thank heavens," said the man, "I thought I'd gone deaf."

I've had a stereo system in my car for years — my wife in front and her mother in the back.

I'm not saying anything against my mother-in-law, but if she lived in India, she'd be sacred.

I met this fellow whose mother-in-law had just died.

"It must be hard to lose a mother-in-law," I consoled him.

"Hard?" he said. "It's almost impossible."

Two golfers were teeing off at the ninth on a golf course near a main road when a funeral procession passed by. One of the golfers stood to attention, doffed his cap and lowered his head.

"That was very considerate of you, old man," said his partner when the procession had passed.

"Not at all," said the other. "She wasn't the worst mother-in-law in the world."

I'm not saying my mother-in-law has a big mouth, but she can give two people the kiss of life at the same time.

Flanigan's house was burned down so he went to the insurance company and demanded money in compensation.

"We don't operate like that, sir," he was told. "What we do is to build a house for you exactly the same as the old one."

"Great heavens," said Flanigan hastily, "in that case cancel the life insurance policy I took out on my mother-in-law!"

Judge: "Are you sure it was your mother-in-law who was driving the car that knocked you down?"

Flanigan: "Of course I'm sure. I'd recognise that laugh anywhere."

Actually, my mother-in-law thinks I'm a god. She must do, because every time she cooks a meal for me she places a burnt offering before me.

A tramp called the other day and my mother-in-law answered the door.

"Any old beer bottles, lady?" he asked cheerfully.

"Do I look like the type to drink beer?" she scowled.

"Any old vinegar bottles lady?" the tramp enquired.

I'm not saying my mother-in-law is a bad cook, but in her house the mice bring their own sandwiches.

My mother-in-law is a noisy eater. Once at a restaurant when she started on her soup, four couples got up and began to dance.

The man at the bar was drowning his sorrows.
"Why so miserable?" asked the barman.
"I had a terrible fight with my mother-in-law," replied the man, tears welling up in his eyes. "She vowed not to speak to me for a whole week."
"That's no reason to be depressed," said the barman. "You should be celebrating a good piece of luck like that!"
"Oh no," said the man, his whole frame racked with sobs. "This happened last week . . . and today's the last day."

My mother-in-law went to have her face lifted, but it didn't work out. The crane broke.

My mother-in-law was married to a travelling salesman, but he took her with him every trip he made. He said he did that rather than have to kiss her good-bye.

I'm not saying my mother-in-law is a bad cook, but South American Indians dip their arrows in her stew.

Flanigan's mother-in-law took ill and was declared dead by the doctor. As the undertaker and his assistants were carrying her downstairs the coffin hit against the bannister and she sat up, large as life and twice as ugly. She recovered fully and lived for thirty more years. Then she was taken ill and again pronounced dead. As they were carrying the coffin down the narrow stairway, Flanigan supervised its progress, saying, "Carefully now lads, very carefully."

When my mother-in-law goes to visit the zoo she has to buy two tickets — one to get in and the other to get out again.

I'm not saying my mother-in-law is ugly, but when she worked as a stripper all the men used to shout, "Put it all back on, put it all back on!"

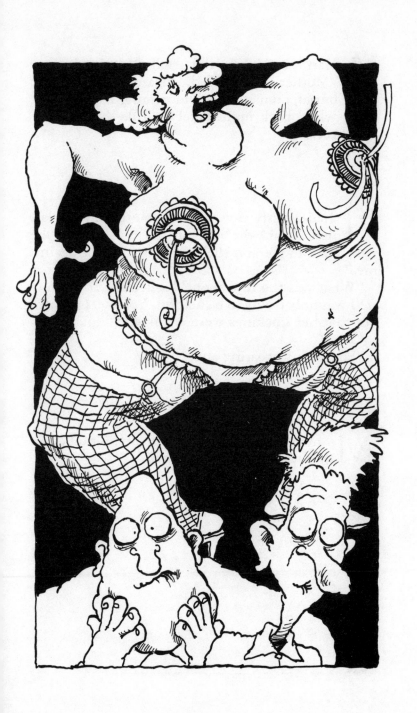

A man received the following telegram: "Mother-in-law dead. Please advise if you want burial, cremation or embalming."

He wired back immediately: "Take no chances. All three."

"I had a nasty row with my mother-in-law last night," said the man in the pub. "Now she won't talk to me and she's turning my wife against me."

"What was the row about?" asked the barman.

"I was only trying to be helpful. You see, I pointed out that her stockings were wrinkled."

"And?"

"She wasn't wearing any."

My mother-in-law can nag the places that other mothers-in-law can't reach.

Whoever made up the proverb "absence makes the heart grow fonder" never met my mother-in-law!

Caspar Milquetoast was enquiring about the job of night security guard at the factory.

The boss looked the delicately-built young man up and down. "The sort we need for this job," he said, "has to be tough, aggressive, fearless, suspicious, distrustful, always on the lookout for trouble and constantly ready to erupt into violence. I just don't think you fit the bill."

"Oh, don't worry about me," explained Caspar. "I've only come to apply for the job on behalf of my mother-in-law."

When my mother-in-law goes on holidays the weather always seems to agree with her — it wouldn't dare not to.

Flanigan: "Do you believe in clubs for mothers-in-law?"

Lanigan: "If all else fails yes — but swing the club hard so she won't be able to fight back."

It was the biggest funeral ever seen — thousands of men marched behind the hearse. At their head was a man with a huge Alsatian dog on a lead.

"Why the dog?" asked a passer-by.

"This is my mother-in-law's funeral," said the man, "and this dog savaged her to death."

"Would it be possible for me to borrow that dog?" asked the passer-by.

"Sure," said the man. "Join the queue."

My mother-in-law is very sensitive though. For example, she won't go to a rugby match because every time there's a scrum she thinks they're all talking about her.

My mother-in-law has such an enormous rear end that when she walks down the street she looks like two little boys fighting under a blanket.

The ancient mother-in-law was sinking fast and seemed to be on the way out.

"I won't be a nuisance to you much longer," she said feebly to her son-in-law.

"Don't worry," said the delighted son-in-law, "of course you will, mother-in-law."

I'm not saying my mother-in-law is ugly, but she uses her lower lip as a bathing cap.

An old dear was at an exhibition of abstract paintings, one of which was painted by her new son-in-law. Asked what she thought of it, she replied, "I've suffered from migraine for years, but I never thought I'd see a picture of it."

It was a wet, stormy day when Murphy buried his mother-in-law. Just as the funeral party left the cemetery there was a sudden flash of lightning and a loud clap of thunder. Murphy looked up at the sky and commented, "Blimey, she's arrived up there already."

I'm not saying my mother-in-law has prominent teeth, but she's the only woman I know who can eat a tomato through a tennis racquet.

The pale-faced man lay on the psychiatrist's couch and began to recount his woes.

"I keep having this ghastly nightmare," he told the psychiatrist. "In it my mother-in-law is chasing me with a bloodthirsty crocodile on a leash. It's terrifying...I see the yellow eyes, the dry scaly skin, the yellow, decaying razor-sharp teeth and smell the foul, heavy breath."

"Sounds disgusting," agreed the psychiatrist.

"That's nothing," the man continued. "Wait till I tell you about the crocodile."

Have you heard about the cannibal who got married and at the wedding reception toasted his mother-in-law?

I'm not saying my mother-in-law is ugly, but she was offered a summer job swimming up and down Loch Ness. Actually, as it turned out it was the first time Nessie had been sighted in decades — picketing the loch.

Finnegan arrived home one night and realised to his horror that his mother-in-law had arrived for a visit. He saw her broomstick in the umbrella rack.

Seriously though, I've developed an attachment for my mother-in-law. It fits over her mouth.

My mother-in-law is such a non-stop talker that when she puts her false teeth in a glass of water at night they don't stop moving for half an hour.

I'm not saying my mother-in-law is ugly, but when she appeared on television they immediately put up a sign: "Please Do Not Adjust Your Set".

"Doctor, I'm worried about my mother-in-law," said the man. "She keeps blowing smoke rings through her nose every time she talks to me. It scares the hell out of me."

The doctor smiled indulgently, saying, "You shouldn't worry about something as trivial as that. A lot of people blow rings when they're smoking."

"That's the whole point," said the man. "She doesn't smoke."

My mother-in-law came home one evening looking much better than usual.

"So you've been to the beauty parlour then," I said to her.

"Beauty parlour nothing," she snarled, "I've just been run over by a bus."

The only way to effectively fight a mother-in-law is with your hat — grab it and run!

One morning my mother-in-law forgot to leave out her rubbish for the garbage men, so as the truck departed she ran after it shouting, "Am I too late?"

"No," they shouted. "Jump in!"

I'm not saying my mother-in-law is a big woman, but once she hung her knickers out on the line to dry and a family of gipsies came along and camped in them.

Flanigan: "I'm the happiest man in the world. I have the finest mother-in-law in the country."
Lanigan: "No wonder you're so happy. Mine lives next door."

My mother-in-law has just bought a dress for a ridiculous figure — and you can't get a figure more ridiculous than hers.

"Dearest heart," said the woman to her husband, "the strangest thing happened the other day. Mother was walking under the clock and it fell off the wall. If it had happened a moment earlier it would have hit mother!"

Her husband replied morosely, "I always thought that clock was slow."

A young man was on trial for murdering his wife.

"You say you accidentally shot your wife," said the judge. "How can that be?"

"That's right," replied the man. "My wife threw herself in front of my mother-in-law just as I pulled the trigger."

I'd love to smother my mother-in-law in diamonds, but there must be a cheaper way.

My mother-in-law was kidnapped last month. We got a note from the kidnappers saying that if we didn't send them the ransom immediately, they would send her back.

"There's something wrong with my car," complained the woman to her son-in-law.

"What's wrong this time?" sighed the man. Her son-in-law was used to this sort of thing.

"I think the engine's flooded."

"All right," said the son-in-law, wearily rising from his chair, "I'll see if I can fix it. Where's the car now?"

"Well, my dear," replied the mother-in-law, "it's still in the river."

What are the four periods of the year when a mother-in-law is at her worst and most difficult to live with?

Spring, summer, autumn and winter.

My mother-in-law does a bit of singing and her voice can charm the birds out of the trees — crows, buzzards, vultures...

Flanigan: "My mother-in-law is an angel."
Lanigan: "You're lucky — mine is still alive."

I'm not saying my mother-in-law has severe varicose veins, but recently she rolled up her skirt and won first prize at a fancy dress competition as a road map. Which was just as well. They were going to give her first prize for the most grotesque mask until they discovered she wasn't wearing one.

There is only one man who is not afraid to tell his mother-in-law where to get off. A bus conductor.

My mother-in-law once complained to the police that I had injured her by banging my head against her steel-tipped boots.

I stuck up for my mother-in-law the other night. Someone said she wasn't fit to mix with pigs and I said she was.

Definition of a gentleman: One who never strikes his mother-in-law except in self-defence.

I've had to ask my mother-in-law not to lean out the window of the car when I'm driving her along. I don't want the police to think I'm driving a horsebox.

It was her first time behind the wheel of a car. "I don't know what to do!" she said nervously.

Said the son-in-law, wearily rubbing his eyes, "Just imagine I'm driving."

Dear old short-sighted Mrs O'Leary, sick in bed, received a visit from, as she thought, the parish priest. After he had left, she told her son-in-law how much she appreciated the priest's kind call.

"But Mother," said the son-in-law, "that wasn't the priest, that was the doctor."

"Oh was it?" replied the old woman. "I thought Father Flanigan was being rather familiar."

Flanigan took his mother-in-law to the seaside last year and they had a lot of fun on the beach burying each other in the sand. This year he's planning to go back and dig her up.

Two golfers were out on the course together, and one of them seemed to be taking an extraordinary amount of trouble with his next drive. His companion asked him why.

"Well," replied the golfer, "I'm very anxious to make this shot a really good one. My mother-in-law came to the course with me today and she's up in the clubhouse watching me."

"Don't be a fool," said his friend. "You haven't got a hope of hitting her from this distance."

I'm not saying my mother-in-law was an ugly baby, but for a month after she was born they were putting the nappy on the wrong end.

The domestic row was in full swing: "I wish," shouted the furious wife, "that I'd taken my mother's advice and not married you!"

"Do you mean to say that your mother tried to prevent you from marrying me?" asked her astonished husband.

"She most certainly did!" snapped the wife.

"My God," whispered the husband, "how I have wronged that woman!"

I'm not saying my mother-in-law is a bad cook, but she's the only woman I know who has an oven that flushes.

"Terribly sorry I'm late," said the panting employee to his irate boss. "My mother-in-law has been staying with us, and this morning she slipped in the bathroom and fell unconscious over the sink."

The boss was instantly sympathetic. "My goodness!" he exclaimed. "What did you do?"

"Well, I didn't know *what* to do at first. Finally I shaved in the bath."

She's not really a big woman, the mother-in-law, but when she hung her bra up on the line to dry last week a camel came along and tried to make love to it. And when she hung her corsets out, they were picketed by people from the "Save the Whale" campaign.

No other animal but man can laugh. He is also the only animal with a mother-in-law.

For thirty years my mother-in-law and I were perfectly happy. Then we met.

A man, his wife and his mother-in-law were journeying through darkest Africa. Suddenly, the wife noticed that her mother was missing. After a frantic search they found her in a small clearing with a lion poised ready to attack her.

"Oh my God, do something!" screamed the wife.

The man considered the situation carefully for a few moments and then said, "Dearest, it looks to me like the lion got himself into this mess. Let him get himself out of it."

I never forget a face — but in my mother-in-law's case I'm willing to make an exception.

"What's the definition of a monologue, Dad?" asked the boy.

"A monologue, my son, is a conversation between a man and his mother-in-law."

When my mother-in-law is driving the car and holds out her hand, you can be sure of three things: she's going to turn left, right or just stop.

I'm not saying my mother-in-law is ugly, but she once paid a visit to the Chamber of Horrors and the attendant said to her, "I'd advise you to keep moving, madam — we're stocktaking."

I went into a bookshop the other day and asked for a book called *How to Control Your Mother-in-law*.

"Our fiction section is upstairs, sir," smiled the assistant.

I'm not saying my mother-in-law is ugly, but when she goes shopping her shadow tries to walk on the other side of the road.

The wife and husband had had a row. The woman's mother was determined to have her say.

"You married my daughter for better or worse!" she screamed, as her son-in-law headed for the door.

"That was four years ago," he yelled back. "When is it going to get better?"

Beauty is only skin deep, as the old proverb goes, but my mother-in-law has inspired another version — ugliness goes all the way through.

I'm not saying my mother-in-law was a peculiar teenager, but of the thirty boys in her class she was the first to shave.

My mother-in-law has threatened to dance on my grave when I die. I'm going to be buried at sea.

I'm not saying my mother-in-law talks too much, but she's the only person I know with a sunburnt tongue.

My mother-in-law's vital statistics are 38-24-38. But not in that order. Actually, she does have a twenty-four-inch waist — that's if you measure her through the centre.

One mother-in-law to another: "I have never made a fool of my son-in-law. I have always given him opportunities to develop his natural capacities."

When my mother-in-law was missing from home for over a month I tried to give her description to the police, but they just wouldn't believe me.

I'm not saying my mother-in-law is fat, but once I was dancing with her for twenty minutes before I realised she was sitting down.

My mother-in-law has just gone on the pill. She doesn't want to have any more grand-children.

This fellow rang the doctor and told him his mother-in-law had lockjaw.

"If you're in this area in the next month or so," he told him, "maybe you could call in and have a look at her."

My mother-in-law just loves nature — and that's really forgiving after what nature did to her.

A mother-in-law died and went to hell. A few days later a knocking was heard on the gates of heaven — it was the devil, looking for political asylum.

Flanigan had a drinking problem so his mother-in-law decided that she would solve it by scaring the wits out of him.

One night when he was drunk, she dressed up in a devil's outfit, complete with horns, cloven hooves and a tail. When Flanigan arrived home, she jumped from behind the front door and shouted, "I'm the devil!"

"Shake hands," said Flanigan. "I'm married to your daughter."

I've just got back from a pleasure trip. I drove my mother-in-law to the airport.

I'm not saying my mother-in-law is a big woman, but she donated one of her bras to a third world charity and they're housing three families in it.

I'm not saying my mother-in-law is ugly, but when she calls round to see us, the mice throw themselves on the traps.

Flanigan: "I've just got a bottle of whiskey for my mother-in-law."
Lanigan: "That's what I call a bargain!"

What is the maximum penalty for bigamy?
Two mothers-in-law.

I'm not saying my mother-in-law is unkind, but during the war she was drummed out of the Gestapo for cruelty.

Seriously though, I've got a soft spot for my mother-in-law. It's a swamp.

Nobody wants my mother-in-law. They've even taken down her picture at the police station.

"You know my mother-in-law can be a bit forgetful sometimes," said Bill. "She fell asleep in the bath with the water running."

"I suppose you must've had a hell of a mess to clean up afterwards," his friend sympathised.

"Well no. She sleeps with her mouth open . . ."

My father-in-law died without saying any last words. His wife was with him to the very end.

My mother-in-law went into a shop to buy a chicken. First she lifted one wing and sniffed underneath, then the other wing. Then she lifted one leg and smelled underneath and then the other leg. Finally, she sniffed the chicken's rear end.

"This chicken isn't fresh," she announced.

"Madam," said the butcher, "would you pass such a test?"

My mother-in-law took a fantastic body-building course. Now she's my father-in-law.

Last week my mother-in-law lost her glasses. She spent half an hour nagging a coat-rack.

I'm not saying my mother-in-law is fat, but she does have bulges in places where other people don't even have places.

The family went on a picnic and the husband took photos. His mother-in-law wasn't very pleased with the shots of her when they were developed.

"They don't do me justice," she complained to her son-in-law.

"Justice," the husband yelped. "You don't want justice, you want mercy."

I haven't spoken to my mother-in-law for years. We haven't fallen out, it's just that I can't manage to interrupt her.

"I'm collecting for the old ladies home," said the charity worker. "Have you anything that you'd like to donate?"

"I certainly have," replied the young husband. "Just wait here and I'll wheel out my mother-in-law."

I'm not saying my mother-in-law is ugly, but when she goes to a professional photographer he puts the black cloth over *her* head.

I'm not saying my mother-in-law is bow-legged, but she's the only woman I know who can walk down a bowling alley without disturbing the game.

The husband smiled pleasantly to his wife on the eve of a visit from her mother.

"It's so nice to see your mother with plenty of get up and go," he said. "Especially when she comes to visit."

Generally speaking, my mother-in-law is generally speaking.

I'm not saying my mother-in-law is a big woman, but she's the only woman I know who can ride a tandem sitting on both saddles at the same time.

What is the ideal tombstone for a mother-in-law?
A heavy one.

A middle-aged woman rushed up the stairs to the church, late for the wedding. An usher stopped her and asked for her invitation.

"I have none," she snapped indignantly.

"Are you a friend of the groom?" asked the usher.

"Certainly not!" replied the woman. "I'm the bride's mother."

One of my mother-in-law's eyes is so beautiful the other eye spends all its time looking at it. Seriously though, her eyes are like pools — football pools, one at home and one away.

How many mothers-in-law does it take to change a light bulb?
A hundred — one to change the light bulb and ninety-nine to say "I told you so".

Explorers report that in some parts of Africa it is the custom for a husband to stand a respectful distance away when addressing his mother-in-law. Where I come from, it's not a custom — it's a safety measure.

I bought my mother-in-law a lovely chair for her birthday, but I just can't get her to plug it in.

Talk about chins — my mother-in-law has five and she's expecting her sixth. She has nearly as many chins as a Chinese telephone directory. She looks as if she's staring at you over a sliced loaf. She needs a bookmark to find her collar.

What's the difference between a mother-in-law and an umbrella?
You can shut up an umbrella.

Mother-in-law: "It's about time mothers-in-law disappeared from joke books."

Son-in-law: "Yes. I think they ought to disappear altogether."